THE FOLLOWER LEADER

LEARNING TO LEAD THE RIGHT WAY

KEMI ADESOLA

THE FOLLOWER LEADER

LEARNING TO LEAD THE RIGHT WAY

KEMI ADESOLA

CONTENTS

DEDICATION

This book is dedicated to the great shepherd, the leader of the universe – JESUS CHRIST who leads us by His blood into the presence of God without blemish.

FOREWORD

BY GORDON ALLAN

L Plates on this side of heaven

I have lived with the phrase "L-Plates on this side of Heaven" for almost 30 years now. They were uttered by my pastor in a sermon during my teenage years and they continue to live with me. I have been in full time Christian ministry for almost 20 years and have some responsibility beyond my church and the denomination that I serve in, however, I still have my "pastor". long time now, I am grateful to God for him as he was willing to take a risk, giving a 16 year -old boy the opportunity to serve, lead and grow in the things of God. I am grateful for his continued wisdom, support, encouragement and influence through the years. Let me ask you, Who are you learning from and in turn who are you leading? Who is speaking into your life and who listens when you speak? In an age of "lifelong learning", when was the last time you intentionally chose to invest in your life and discipleship journey? To develop your leadership skills, I would suggest that you need to constantly lead yourself. "L plates" has become something of a confession and an inspiration in my life and ministry. It offers a grounding that keeps me humble before God and man. It reminds me that I haven't "arrived" and that I am in desperate need of the Lord's Grace, at the same time, it spurs me on to greatness and adventures in God. There is more to learn, more to experience and more opportunities to be guided by the Holy Spirit into situations where I can display and demonstrate the love of our heavenly Father to a hurting world. The great commission (*Matthew 28:18-20*) makes it clear that "making disciples" is not an optional extra for any follower of Christ. It is heaven's heartbeat for you and I, whether we are leaders, followers or hopefully both! Every learner driver looks forward to the day when they can remove the "L- plates" from the car as they are deemed fit and competent, having passed the test. For you and I as Jesus' followers, we look forward to hearing those words "well done good and faithful servant" (*Matthew 25:23*). The Bible context is of servants who have been faithful with the master's resources. They have been given a trust, in this case financial, and in the master's absence are to put the talent(s) to good use. Their faithfulness in their steward-ship was the key to increased respon-sibility as they stepped into their future. he Biblical principle is that "you have been faithful with a few things. I will put you in charge of many things." This flies in the face of the instant celebrity culture that reality TV and YouTube has generated over the last 15 years. We live in a world where anyone can become a "superstar" overnight. There is no partic-ular sense of the relevance of training, developing, maturing, apprenticeship or learning the ropes. Often the influences of the world can creep into churches and our leader/ follower relationships.

There was a reason why David's public reign as a King was preceded by his private life as a Shepherd boy. His greatest battle against the Philistine Giant Goliath (*1Samuel 17:1-58*) relied upon the lessons he had previously learned from God when no one else was around. Those lessons were included over-coming fear, facing opposition (lion and bear) and stewardship rather than running away to preserve his own life at the expense of his father's sheep.

Those "hidden valley moments" set Da-vid up for his public moment when the eyes, hopes and freedom of the nation were upon him. The world is still watching and looking for authentic men and women of God who have learned to trust God, over-come opposition while remaining in right relation-ship with God and man. Set your personal discipleship "bar" high. Whatever you give place to in your life, you can expect those around you to give place to it in theirs; lifestyle, language, habits and behaviours, including the good, the bad and the holy.

In fact your bottom line will become your followers' top line. Whatever you do others will aspire to achieve in theirs. If those who are following you model their lives on your life, how healthily will they grow? It impresses me that David made it clear that he came against Goliath in "the name of the Lord Almighty, the God of the armies of Israel" He wasn't fighting for his own prominence.

It impresses me that when he is brought before the King after the battle that he identifies himself as both a "son" and a "servant." If we could go through our life and ministries with that healthy balance of being a son who is loved and led and a servant who bows before his king in our case, God but blesses others through actions and attitudes, we will become those that the Lord can trust with promotion and position. The Lord Jesus wasn't lost for words too often, but Matthew records in his gospel that Jesus "was astonished" (*Matthew 8:10*) at the faith and insight that a Roman centurion communicated.

His servant was ill and he brought his plight to the attention of the Lord, but, when Jesus offers to go to his home to pray for the servant he refuses.

The Centurion indicates that he doesn't deserve Jesus to come to his home. He confesses that if Jesus speaks the word his servant would be healed because he understood the power of the command and authority behind it. The servant's healing resulted because of the Centurion's faith. This man of authority humbles himself on behalf of one under his own authority in order that a great-er authority (Jesus' healing command) might be released. Being under authority teaches important faith growing principles that allows you to step into a moment where lessons are learnt, lives are transformed, and the Lord's commendation comes your way. This Centurion knew that although he was a leader in every other arena of his life, in this moment before Jesus he had to be the follower.

Our leader/ follower relationship with the Lord is developed based on direction and devotion. He offers His response is devotion towards Him. Sadly, too often today Christians flip that on its head. We think that our relationship with Jesus is that He will bless whatever direction we want our lives to go and that we will still be assured of His devotion. Jeremiah 6:16 says "stand at the crossroads and look; ask for the ancient paths, ask where the good way is and walk in it and you will find rest for your souls." The chapter goes on to speak about a people who don't walk the ancient paths and who reap the consequence of their unwillingness to follow the Lord's direction.

Please don't be one of those people who think that God will give a "big thumbs up" and bless whatever direction, attitude or behaviour you display. Even a competent "L plate" driver still needs an instructor in the car with Him. Driving Instructors give direction and ensure that the developing driver and those around them are safe and free from harm in the moment. They also teach the principles required to be competent behind the wheel for the rest of your driving life. I am grateful for the driving instructor who grabbed the wheel as I misjudged my left turn at a set of traffic lights. My line of direction was wrong and I was going to cause an accident. To worsen matters, someone from my office was sitting in the queue of cars that I was heading towards.

Yes, others heard about it the next day...As I reflect upon that moment now, I realise that part of the "L plate" lesson is our ability to take correction. My driving instructor was on my side, he wanted to train me to pass (I did 1st time!), wanted to commend my successes, develop my skills but would also point out my errors and would certainly prevent potential accidents that his experience could foresee. Build people into your life who can lead, encourage and correct you well. Have some friends who know you well enough and who won't believe your own publicity, the Bible teaches that "faithful are the wounds of a friend" (Proverbs 27:6) and just a few verses after that Scripture declares that "as iron sharpens iron so one person sharpens another" (Proverbs 27:17). It might just be that someone cares for you enough to bring a correction to your life that prevents immediate disaster but that also puts you on a path of safety for years to come. This in turn becomes a principle that you share with others who follow you and your example. Be an Iron sharpener. Have you ever tried to cut bread or meat with a blunt knife?

It is not easy, and the presentation is not aid-ed by such an implement! What if we looked on our leader follower relationships in the same way a Michelin Star Chef takes care of his best carving knife? We have all seen the sight of a chef running the cutting edge of a chopping knife along a sharpening steel. The result of this preparation process makes all the difference to the public presentation. Private moments of good questions, encouragements and challenges can sharpen and develop those around us. It is vital that there are strong relationships in place, that permission to speak into each other's lives have been given and that the conversation is always laced with grace. This does not mean that we look for opportunities to "pull people up, " highlighting every and any fault with relish and delight! Any correction should not be with a view to punish but to bring restoration and refinement to the area of weakness. We are not called to beat up but to build up for the Kingdom of God! Sometimes the best lessons are learnt through reflecting and learning through our failures. In those moments the leader needs to be able to come alongside, strengthen, support, ask specific questions and offer spiritual perspective. This should only be done after a time of spiritual ocular surgery. The Bible advises one to "first take the plank out of your own eye, and then you will see clearly to remove the speck from your brother's eye" (**Matthew 7:5**).

I have felt the momentary discomfort of an eyelash that I can blink away. I have also felt the eye watering effect of a piece of grit in my eye that required a visit to the hospital, the skill of a doctor and a longer period of recovery before 20/20 vision was restored. I didn't enjoy either, but I was grateful afterwards, clear vision is always helpful. I continue to wear my "L-plates" with a sense of aspiration and pride.

I am thankful to those who allowed me to walk with them in life and ministry. They were further on than me, yet they slowed their pace for me to catch up and eventually step up in ministry. I am grateful or the lessons learned and the opportunity given. I now do my best to encourage others to grow, develop and flourish in the things of God. I do so in the knowledge that there is much more learning, following and leading this side of heaven. In that sense I am a follower- leader.

Pastor Gordon Allan, Senior Leader,
Elim Pentecostal Church, Edinburgh

"The challenge of leadership is to be strong, but not rude; be kind, but not weak; be bold, but not bully; be thoughtful, but not lazy; be humble, but not timid; be proud, but not arrogant; have humor, but without folly."

Jim Rohn (1930-2009)

"Everything rises and falls on leadership".
John. C. Maxwell.

INTRODUCTION

"And God said to Abraham leave your native country, your relatives, and your father's family, and go to the land that I will show you"-
(Genesisi12:1)

Jesus said to His disciples, "follow me and I will make you fishers of men"- (Matthew 4:19)

Paul said to the Corinthians "follow me as I follow Christ" – (1st Corinthians 11:1)

Many books have been written about leader-ship, the responsibilities, skills and challenges.

Perhaps nothing more or new could be said or written about leadership but to remind our generation constantly that whatever we are lacking or missing in any place or situation can always be traced to leadership, there can be no real progress until there is real leadership.

In the market place, evidence is show-ing that the success of any good company depends heavily on leadership and how it is employed to drive innova-tion and people talent.

No great business plan will ever make much impact until a great leader steps in to drive the initiative. That is why the Chief Executive Officer of a company may receive a bigger salary because they are paid to take the lead.

Nations, organisations and even churches are real-ising the power of leadership and its influences on success rate. A lot is riding on leadership any-where and everywhere. Much of good leadership skills can be passed on from one generation to another through intentional mentoring and learner follower-ship. Even biblical heroic leaders were great follow-ers. In my humble opinion, the best method of growing leaders is by teaching them to observe and follow. If you can't follow well, you can't lead well. Until we start following with intention, there will be no lasting impact on our generation because custom gets passed from one generation to another mainly through observation and apprenticeship formally or informally.

Parents pass life lessons to their children as they live their lives before them and show them examples of skills, good values and actions. Wihout adequate mentorship, leadership may experience limitations, undue hardship and unmitigated failures. "Follower-ship is a product of buying into the truth of your leader, it is unfortunate that we seem to have a generation of independent people who have not learnt from others who have been ahead of them. David followed Saul, Elisah followed Elijah, Joshua followed Moses. Who are you following?"- Bishop David. O. Oyedepo.

Leadership skills can be taught and learned throughout our life-time, a learning attitude and a teachable heart, who can resist?

I must be seen.

I must do what everybody likes.

I must be heard.

I must be available all the time.

I must be perfect.

I must solve everybody's problem.

Contrary to some opinions, leadership is not a tool of oppression and certainly not to be used as a measure of seniority. It is the ability to inspire, direct skills, resources and potentials of people towards progressive life outcomes for them and those around them, it is not do as I say but do as I do. "Leaders with Character do not set themselves above the people, they roll up their sleeves, get involved and show the way. Those of us who are leaders are the models, the ones people look to as examples, so we must live in a way that is worthy of the high calling of leadership. This is not about perfection, it's about having a heart that is sold out to a godly way of life". - Dan Reiland

Leadership is a movement of the Heart. "Keep your heart with all diligence for out of it flows the issues of life"- (*Proverbs 4:23*)

When your heart moves a gear up more than the next person close to you, your eyes begin to see things differently and you pursue purpose deliberately. The heart is the engine room of all actions. Nothing gets done except it has been purposed from the heart. Many people imagine that they deserve to be in a leadership position or possess the useful skills and capacity for it and they strive, push, lobby for the post only to discover that it is more than what they bargained for. They are not prepared for the emotional, physical and social challenges that comes with leadership. In contrast, a follower leader learns on the job. For Christian leaders, followership is essential as demonstrated by a popular teaching of our lord Jesus Christ in (*Mark 10: 42-44*).

Jesus called his disciples and told them, "you know that those who are recognized as rulers among the unbelievers lord it over them, and their superiors act like tyrants over them. That's not the way it should be among you.

Instead, whoever wants to become great among you must be your servant, and whoever wants to be first among you must be a slave to everyone."

Leadership is not a position, it is a matter of the heart because we are serving people, but we hold a leadership position at least from a Christian stand-point. Leaders are to maintain an understanding and attitude of service through following the people ahead of them because a lot is riding on the leader/follow-er relationship. Many lessons will not be passed on until a person decides to follow another person intentionally. Leading usually starts with the heart and leadership without the heart can result in tyranny.

Instead, whoever wants to become great among you must be your servant, and whoever wants to be first among you must be a slave to everyone."

Leadership is not a position, it is a matter of the heart because we are serving people, but we hold a leadership position at least from a Christian stand-point. Leaders are to maintain an understanding and attitude of service through following the people ahead of them because a lot is riding on the leader/follow-er relationship. Many lessons will not be passed on until a person decides to follow another person intentionally. Leading usually starts with the heart and leadership without the heart can result in tyranny.

Leadership is about building and rebuild-ing, hearts, character, people, visions and purposes. Ezra was such a leader, he was moved in his heart to lead the rebuilding in his days.

"In the first year of Cyrus king of Persia, in order to fulfil the word of the Lord spoken by Jeremiah, the Lord moved the heart of Cyrus king of Persia to make a proclamation through-out his realm and also to put it in writing:

This is what Cyrus king of Persia says: "The Lord, the God of heaven, has given me all the king-doms of the earth and he has appointed me to build a temple for him at Jerusalem in Judah. Any of his people among you may go up to Jerusalem in Judah and build the temple of the Lord, the God of Israel, the God who is in Jerusalem, and may their God be with them. And in any locality where survivors may now be living, the people are to pro-vide them with silver and gold, with goods and live-stock, and with freewill offerings for the temple of God in Jerusalem." Then the family heads of Judah and Benjamin, and the priests and Levites— everyone whose heart God had moved— prepared to go up and build the house of the Lord in Jerusalem. All their neighbours assisted them with articles of silver and gold, with goods and livestock, and with valuable gifts, in addition to all the freewill offerings". – (*EZRA 1: 1- 6*)

Balanced Leadership

The need for a balanced leadership has been a challenge for generations, in the secular world and especially in religious circles. popular or trendy leadership styles are taking the concepts of leadership from one generation and attempting to pass the tradition to another without considering that times are changing, roles are reversing, and the digital world is slowly creating an individualistic person out of us all. It is becoming apparent that our generation needs capable leaders because of the huge confusion and chaos that abound in our days. Churches, governments and organisations are desperate for sound leadership.

I was raised in Christ Apostolic Church in Nigeria and we were taught the rudiments of the bible from a young age and I still support the doctrinal teachings that were passed to us because we were trained to regard leaders, obey them but to also read our bibles and hold onto a strong faith in Christ continually. When I began to attend charismatic Pentecostal churches, I was alarmed at the amount of disruption, rebellion and lack of disciplined commitment that was common.

Unruly social and sexual behaviours among men and women, which should not take place among Christians because the bible is clear about acceptable behaviours in these areas. I also observed a lack of discipline among church volunteers who claim to love Christ and yet avoid prayer meetings, outreach gatherings, have little discussion on sanctification and avoid talks on accountability and punctuality to name a few. I prayed about my discoveries and I got an inspiration from the story of Samuel in (1 Samuel 3). I concluded that the best thing any leader could do for his followers is to train them by communicating the pure teachings of the bible and for the leader and followers to educate one another about the fear of the lord and live a life with a pure conscience. No denomination is presented as being better than others here by any means, but leaders of all Christian denominations will help us a great deal if sound and loving biblical teachings and guidelines are brought back to our churches in order to raise a generation of followers with a heart to build.

Slay Your Giants! – Emotions

Emotions are a basic part of us humans, it is the

part of us that connects with others on a deeper level negatively or positively. As leaders, we still carry human emotions as any other person. The key is not to remove emotions from our decision-making process or to pursue some robotic form of existence. Instead, we must learn to deal with those emotions in a productive way. Identify how your feelings affect your thinking. For instance, rage and fear can move you to act against an unacceptable set of circumstances which, is good, but, those feelings let on the loose can cause major damage to you and those you care about.

By learning to acknowledge your feelings, and even embrace them, you begin to build aware-ness of them. Take time to see how those feelings change and how this influences your actions.

Once you understand how emotions affect you and your thought process, you can begin learning how other people's emotions affect them. As you gain ability to see things from their perspective, you will also gain ability to communicate in a way they under-stand. Those abilities can help increase the quality of your interactions with others and help you build stronger relationships. In the end, the goal is simple:

a. Make emotions work for you instead of against you.

b. Think for yourself by yourself.

c. Ask relevant and timely questions about life issues.

d. Base your judgements on checked facts from authorised sources.

e. Pray well before making a life changing decision.

f. Adopt more practical methods to life issues.

2

The fear of God

"The fear of God reigning in the heart is the beauty of the soul"- Matthew Henry (1662-1714)

Leadership is about people. Lead with knowledge and the fear of God. The goal of spiritual leadership is to see that people come to know God, to glorify him in all that they do, to esteem Him above all and fear Him totally. When any of these attributes are missing in a leader or the followers, there will be anarchy and division. Every leader should conduct a heart MOT regularly. Keep your heart away from spoilers, allow God only to get close because He alone knows what we are.

"If you are a pastor, a missionary, or serve in a church, you can't avoid discouragement, disappointment, or hurt from ministry. The bible even uses the not-so-complimentary metaphor "sheep" to describe those we serve. Sheep get dirty and smelly and often kick and bite. Sometimes those sheep in the church do the same to their shepherds. So, when you get kicked, forgotten, dis-respected, ignored, mistreated, gossiped about, or misunderstood, how do you move forward?

The story recorded in *1 Samuel 30* gives great insight. David had just begun his career to fight the bad guys. Earlier, he faced a huge defeat. While he and his army were in battle far from home, the bad guys, the Amalekites, attacked the city where his family and the families of his army lived. They burned the city and kidnapped their wives and children. When David's men discovered this, they considered removing him from his position, not by a vote of a board or a congregation, but with big rocks to the head by stoning him possibly to death.

The Scriptures then record one of the most beautiful verses ever written. The King James Version captures it well:

David encouraged himself inthe Lord his God. (*1 Sam. 30:6*)

It worked because his guys didn't stone him but

marshalled their energy and once again pursued the bad guys under his leadership. As I have faced discouragement in ministry, these simple choices have helped me encourage myself in the Lord.

a. Acknowledge your pain and emotion to the Lord, but don't wallow in it.
b. Journal your thoughts. Writing them down helps me stop the tendency to incessantly mull over the hurtful situation.
c. Read God's word, especially those verses that speak of hope and victory.

d. Do something pro-active. Take action to move forward. In David's case he took specific action to resolve the problem. He rallied his troops to chase down the Amalekites.
e. Stop condemning yourself and remind yourself that you are a child of God, loved by Him with great intrinsic value regardless of whether your church is growing or whether people treat you with respect. f. Pray for those who have hurt you. I'm amazed how God defuses looming bitterness in my heart when I pray for the sheep that bite me.

"If you get knocked down, sincerely seek the Lord and rise up in His strength to begin anew" - Charles Stone.

Leadership and Meditation

Meditation is the process of quieting the mind to spend time in thought. Reflection is similar, but the difference is that reflection takes place after a situation or action has occurred to review the effects of such and how to perform better if a similar situation happens. Meditation focuses on matters both occurring and imagined. The chances of meditation leading to worry and anxiety is very high if uncontrolled and without a good focus.

There are no right or wrong ways of meditation but the goal or focus of meditation is the only way to check if it is profitable or not. If a leader meditates on his mistakes all the time, he will become fearful and hesitant. If he also meditates on his strong points only, he may lose self-awareness, hate criticism even when it is constructive and become difficult. In meditation, our soul is led to a destination either good or bad. When we meditate on the word of God, we reap the life-giving benefits and the holy spirit activates the creative force in us deposited by God. The mind of the leader is one of their greatest assets – out of it proceeds plans and motives for carrying out the leadership vision and it is the seat of life's battles as winning or losing begins in the mind.

Any battle lost in the mind is totally lost.

Our mind is the seat of all intellectual deci-sions and in the final analysis every assessment of life situation resides solely in the mind of the person doing the assessment. "As a man thinketh in His heart so is he" – Proverbs 23:7 If a leader is fervent about their mission, they need to care for their mind. "Summing it all up, friends, do your best by filling your minds and meditating on things true, noble, reputable, authentic, compelling, gracious—the best, not the worst; the beautiful, not the ugly; things to praise, not things to curse. Put into practice what you learned from me, what you heard and saw and real-ized. Do that, and God, who makes everything work together, will work you into his most excellent harmonies". – (**Phillipians 4:8**). According to dictio-nary .com "our mind has been defined as the element of a person that enables them to be aware of the world and their experiences, the way we think and feel. It is a person's ability to reason". Our minds are mirrors, it reflects, copies, shows attitudes and gives feedbacks. Out of the mind proceeds decisions, plans, choices, conclusions and assumptions.

We become as we think, and our thoughts are silent speeches. It is interesting to note that our mind is a rare gift from God.

"God did not give us a spirit of timidity or coward-ice or fear, but He has given us a spirit of power and of love and of sound judgment and personal discipline [abilities that result in a calm, well balanced mind and self-control". – (*2 Timothy 1:7*).

Our minds are actively calculating and never stops processing ideas images and plans. The bible some-times describes it as our heart or understanding.

"Be careful of your thoughts, they may become words at any moment" - Lara Glassen

There are many things that proceeds out of our minds but most of them are issues we deliberately put in there. By hearing, watching or participating in activities, we involve our minds in one form or another. Our minds are both physical organs in form of, the brain and a deeper spiritual element called "the sub- conscious mind". The latter is more powerful because it can continue to operate even when the physical mind, our brain is resting through sleep or rest. This might be one of the reasons why some sleep people and have others a have good night nightmares.

The bible warns us to "guard our hearts diligently" and this means to protect anything from sinking into the deeper parts of our minds. The only item we should allow to be deeply buried into our subconscious mind is the word of God. Our mind can be strong or weak. It can be easily led astray or confused depending on what we expose ourselves to.

To lose one's mind is the inability to exert a considerable influence over our thought process. Our mind can be con-trolled through self- discipline and constant prayer.

The famous writer William James said "The greatest weapon against stress is our ability to choose one thought over another"

How can I control my thoughts? Imagine your thoughts are being recorded and will be played out in public. What will you think about?

Care Of The Mind

As new born in Christ, our minds remain in an old state and we need the reprogramming of what has been planted in us from childhood through cultural perceptions, biases, prejudices and views or even weak religious doctrines.

Our minds should be actively engaged with bible reading and challenging the obstacles that are stacked up in there through meditating on scriptures and confessing the word of God loudly and boldly.

Practical steps to keep a healthy mind include:

a. Writing down your thoughts in a diary – this relieves the pressure we put on our brain.
b. Make a goal to speak to a trusted person at least once a month.

c. Declutter your personal commitments, don't get involved in matters that you have no power to solve.

d. Recognise your limitations and don't over stretch yourself.
e. Sleep well and make your bedroom tidy.
f. Pray before you got to bed. (some people only do morning prayers).
g. Put a note on your bedroom wall that says, "God is my helper" (or write the one you prefer).

In an article by Richard D. Dobbins, he admitted that after years of trying to please church members, he concluded that the church is filled with difficult people who are damaged either emotionally or spiritually sometimes in more than two areas.

"As a pastor, I found getting along with these few people to be one of my greatest challenges.

Learning to deal with them effectively required me, first, to face my own unrealistic expectations of them. I expected these people to be spiritual rather than carnal. However, through the years I have come to realize that believers are more likely to be carnal than they are to be spiritual. This has always been true of the church. After all, most of the books of the new testament address carnal issues among first century Christians. Had these believers been spiritual, these books would be missing from our Bible. Second, I expected these difficult people, along with every other person in the church, to love me. Somehow, I thought I was failing in my ministry if I could not earn the love of every person in the church. This, too, was another unrealistic expectation.

There is no church where the pastor is loved by everyone. At any given moment, 10 to 20 percent of any congregation would prefer someone else as their pastor. Learning to accept this as normal frees the pastor from the bondage of compulsively seeking to be loved by every person in the church.

People pick offence at leaders for various reasons, from common aggravations to huge incidents that spiral out of control, but the main enemy of the church is the devil, the slanderer so when the devil is about to attack a church, slander is the main weapon.

Bitterness clouds people's sense of judgement and emotional balance. We begin to see issues from our own perspective alone and ignore the global effects that our actions might create. Bitterness is a state of the heart, a mirror of what is going on in the inner mind. Conflicts and criticism is a great window of opportunity to check and confirm how people feel about you but con-sider the motives of such comments if it is target-ed to shut you up, ignore it and speak louder".

Expecting Persecution

Persecution is a big part of the Chritian life package, remember Jesus. "He came to His own and his own received him not, but for them that receive Him he gave the pow-er to become the son of God". – (*John 1:11-12*). Many people around you may not like you but there are people out there who want to hear you, spread your wings and fly. Persecution hides life lessons any follower leader who is willing to learn must see persecution as a road to victory because even the Apostle were able to spread the message of the gospel due to persecution. Jesus Christ had to borrow a boat to preachhe asked for a colt to be untied so he can ride to Jerusalem, and even begged for fish and bread to feed the 5000. When any man is resisting persecution, he is not fir for the Kingdom of God.

3

Following Instructions.

It is safe to say that of all the commands that God gives to His people, especially leaders, nothing is as abstract to us as the command to fear Him because the word of God is filled with scriptures that advise us not to fear nor be afraid. There-fore, when we encounter the concept of the fear of the Lord, it sounds like an enigmatic advice in-tended to confuse us, however, God's intention to us is clear. His fear is not fearsome but a source of life and wisdom. Moses didn't possess a huge amount of this fear because in (Exodus chapter 2) he committed a blunder even though he was destined to lead the Israelites out of slavery. Killing an Egyptian in haste to defend the Israelites exposed his lack of fear for God and how little he valued human life.

Moses was chosen by God from birth to exe-cute His plan of freedom to the captive nation of Israel, but Moses lacked this intrinsic character called the fear of the lord and God had to show him dramatic events to establish godly fear in him. The burning bush the signs before Pharaoh, the ten plagues and the red sea events were all God's plan to instil this fear into the innermost parts of Moses because he was to receive the leadership of a whole nation and lead them to the promised land which was a different assignment from their liberation from Egypt.

This intrinsic capacity is vital to leaders because without it errors will be made, and potential disaster could occur. In a similar example from the bible, Moses went up to receive the tablets from God on the mount. After fasting for 40 days and nights, seeing the glory of God, basking in God's presence he came back to discover that Aaron had been mentoring the people in idolatry practices even though he didn't take the full responsibility to explain how the golden calf appeared.

Aaron gave an incredible excuse for this blatant disobedience to God's first commandment to His children. "Do not be angry, my lord," Aaron answered. "You know how prone these people are to evil. They said to me, 'Make us gods who will go before us. As for this fellow Moses who brought us up out of Egypt, we don't know what has happened to him.' So, I told them, 'Whoever has any gold jewellery, take it off.' Then they gave me the gold, and I threw it into the fire, and out came this calf!" Moses saw that the people were running wild and that Aaron had let them get out of control and so become a laughingstock to their enemies. So, he stood at the entrance to the camp and said,

"Whoever is for the LORD, come to me."And all the Levites rallied to him.

Then he said to them, "This is what the LORD, the God of Israel, says: Each man straps a sword to his side. Go back and forth through the camp from one end to the other, each killing his brother and friend and neighbour"- (*Exodus 32:21-27*). Moses repeated the actions he took in Egypt when he killed one Egyptian thinking he was defending a just cause but this time it was genocide not homicide. The fear of the lord was not gripping Moses' heart enough at this stage, so, he kept going back to the school that God set up for him to learn to fear God ultimately.

Moses feared God greatly, but, it was based mainly on the extrinsic features of the personality and acts of God that created the fear for Moses not the inner godly fear that is required to redeem our soul.

Leaders need to develop a godly fear that recognises the sovereignty of God and the redeeming capacity of His grace towards all men and follow this grace daily in our lives and assignments. The fear of the lord saves from destruction. Joseph saved his generation from hunger because he recognised the omnipresence of God and he exhibited this in his daily affairs even when no-body was watching him with Potiphar's wife.

Leaders are moulded in secret, what you do when nobody is watching is what you really are.

"Tremble, earth, at the presence of the Lord, at the presence of the God of Jacob, who turned the rock into a pool". – *Psalms 114:7.* Many people avoid leadership positions because of criticism and rejection from others but they deny themselves the opportunity to enrol in the school of destiny. Something is always at stake, when destiny is bubbling inside you. To deny it is to deny the truth.

Leadership and Emotional Intelligence

Emotion has been defined as a strongfeeling derived from someone's circumstances, mood or relationship with others. We can begin to understand others only when we are able to interpret our own emotions.

The exercises below are tools designed to check emotional responses to life situations:
circle your own response and reflect on them

(1) When someone upsets me, try to hide my feelings. **True/False**

(2) If someone pushed me, I would push back. **True/False**

(3) I remember things that upset me or make me angry for a long time afterwards. **True / False**

(4) I seldom feel irritable. **True/False**

(5) I often take chances crossing the road. **True / False**

(6) People find it difficult to tell whether I'm excited about something or not. **True / False**

(7) I often do or say things I later regret. **True / False**

(8) I find it difficult to comfort people who have been upset. **True / False**

(9) I generally don't bear a grudge - when something is over, it's over, and I don't think about it again. **True/False**

(10) No one gets one over on me, I don't take things lying down. **True/ False**

(11) When something upsets me, I prefer to talk to someone about it than to bottle it up. **True / False**

(12) I have been involved in many fights or arguments. **True/False**

(13) I get 'worked up' just thinking about things that have upset me in the past. **True / False**

(14) I'm not easily distracted. **True / False**

Emotional care for leaders and followers are essential to growth and stability because our soul is the seat of desires, longings and dreams it is a garden that needs to be tended. only those with the plan to care for their soul and take active steps to protect and nourish it.

Leadership And Self-Care

Self-care has been described as "the actions that an individual might take in order to reach optimal physical spiritual and mental health". For church leaders who are serving in multiple capacities and roles, It is imperative for us to be self-aware and keep a good eye on for our all-round wellness. We need to nurture our spirit, soul and body while recognising that it is scriptural and godly to live a balanced Christian life.

Since our spiritual self is what we give as instruments of healing to people, if we are sick or tired we can't help others effectively nor serve God meaningfully.

God is the only omnipotent and sovereign who neither sleeps nor slumber. we as humans however will be so we need periods of rest.

if we are sick or tired we can't help others effectively nor serve God meaningfully.

Jesus had to depart several times to rest and he always invited His disciples to come to "the other side". A place of rest not only physically but mentally and emotionally. Jesus spoke to the multitudes in parables and explained to His disciples later as a means of assisting them to reach their full potential and taking time to reflect. To have a successful balanced Christian life we need to practice self-care regularly because as leaders we are vulnerable to Over commitment, Burnout, Fatigue, Stress, Illness.

Steps to a Successful Self-care approach
a. *Setting good boundaries early*

b. *Listen to your body*

c. *Find out what restores you, it's different for everybody.*

d. *Be careful of the statement, "I am always available", we are not God.*

e. *Give yourself permission to feel good.*

f. *Inform your team about rest days or times.*

g. *Nurture yourself in the following 3 ways*
Good nutrition for the body
Good play and laughter for the soul
prayer, good books, seminars e.t.c for the spirit

h. *Keep a journal for progress and development.*

i. Exercise moderately and regularly.

j. Keep and connect with good friends not only on social media but meeting up when possible.

k. Have a good reflection pattern not rumination.

l. Protect your prayer life from distractions e.g. phones and emails.

m. Don't ignore warning signs from your body e.g. persistent headaches, body pains, feelings of irritations towards people without a reasonable cause.

n. Understand that rest is not a sin (Sleep is different from rest).

o. Plan and go for an affordable holiday.

Remember to think and meditate about this point: While we are helping others, who is helping us? Who is helping the person helping us?

Could you think of 5 people that can help you with what ever you do as a leader?

Every person is RESPONSIBLE for self-care.

In conclusion every person is RESPONSIBLE for

self-care; let us begin the culture of our spiritual mental and physical health NOW!

Men may pretend and make you believe they are thinking of you and praying for you but truth be told, God has the best plans for us and we receive those plans as we obey instructions.

"For I know the plans I have for you, declares the lord, plans for welfare and not for evil, to give you a future and a hope"- (*Jeremiah 29:11*)

According to John Piper "If you want to be a great leader of people you have to learn to get away from people to be with God regularly".

Leadership and Divine Promises

God gave Joshua an assignment and a commandment to lead people to the promise land after the death of Moses and Joshua obeyed with zeal and excitement armed with plenty of the promises from God alone and that was enough for him anyway.

God promised him victory everywhere he led the Israelites to either in battle or to dwell. Joshua fought many battles in his time, but he never lost sight of the promises of God. When God sends His word, it will not remove your battle as a follower or leader because when it's time to conquer any area of our lives, the former occupant will not give up without a fight. Our antennae must be constantly tuned to battle and victory at the same time, so that hopelessness will not take over. We must stand against rebellion, in prayer and in confrontation. The battles we fight in our days are not too different from the days of Joshua in the bible but ours is a moral battle as well as spiritual, the moral decline is currently creeping into the church, so the battle is becoming an internal warfare. The wisdom of the world cannot be al-lowed in the house of God – it is demonic. It is safe to point out here that many cultures that are being allowed in today's church is not per-missive to the ethics of the bible. The church is not a cultural centre so the only acceptable culture in the church as prescribed by the scriptures is to love and serve God in humility and purity.

4

_____

To do and Teach

"Lead, Follow or get out of theway"
  –LaurenceJ.Peter(1919-1990)

Success in leadership is not an option. Some-one must lead, others need to follow diligently or there will be chaos and anarchy. God doesn't do democracy. In every community, good lead-ing is the key to progress and most times some followers assume that leaders can be correct-ed by just giving them advice which they should follow instantly especially in the church setting.

I support the idea of followers giving advice to leaders but what I strongly oppose is any advice that is given without due consultation as to their usefulness and application and of course we must consider the authenticity and the person of the adviser.

For instance, a member of the church that does not contribute or support the group financially and pro-poses projects or give financial advice expecting every body to follow that suggestion may be assuming the wrong position because you need to say and do just to be a good example of a follower of Christ who always showed people what to do by doing it Himself.

"In the first book, o Theophilus, I have dealt with all that Jesus began to do and teach" (Acts 1:1)

The Excellent Leader

According to the Cambridge English dictionary, 'Excellence' is described as "the quality of being outstanding or extremely good." Joshua was extremely good, he was almost better than Moses, he saw potential in problems and was ready to solve them That explains why Joshua conquered more lands than Moses. A follower leader filled with an excellent spirit will have no time for betrayal and disloyalty because these traits will rob a man of his creativity and vision. Betrayal is a deliberate disloyalty, with intent to mislead and deceive.

Many followers and leaders who have betrayal tendencies which represents an innate pride originating from the devil find it hard to follow others because it appears to be a waste of time to a leader who is not a follower at heart. This attribute might explain the proliferation of religious groups all over the world today.

Betrayal in Leadership

Acts of betrayal usually takes place when the follower feels or think too highly of themselves or have an over estimation of their capacity.

In the bible, several cases of betrayal are recorded, and they never end well.

Consider Mordecai and Haaman, two biblical historical characters, both were servants to the king, but one felt esteemed more than the other and wanted respect at all costs. When Haman saw that Mordecai would not kneel or pay him honour he was enraged. Yet having learned who Mordecai's people were, he scorned the idea of killing only Mordecai. Instead Haman looked for a way to destroy all Mordecai's people, the Jews, throughout the whole kingdom of Xerxes - (*Esther 3:5-6*).

When some followers are slighted they can go to any length to prove their point until they create a distraction from the group's main purpose. In the story above, Mordecai sought the help of a queen, Esther who happens to be a follower at heart and she was able to rescue her generation through her humility and loyalty. Have no fear of opposition when you stand for godly values. Let no one suggest to you that you are not good enough, every-one has a rough edge, God straightens us out in His own time. The reality of being a moral and ethical leader is that life is always a function of copy. People copy what they see. Lead with a clear fo-cus and a well -developed value system, learn to determine right from wrong, good from bad and be open to value-based learning. When you walk with God, live like a photographer, focus "forget-ting those things which are behind and straining forward to what lies ahead"- (*Phillipians 3:13b*).

Leadership and Resourcefulness

According to Dictinary.com, an online resource material, resourcefulness is defined as the ability and creativity to cope with difficulties. It is being able to deal well with new or difficult situations and to find solutions to problems. It is also the ability to act effectively or imaginatively in difficult circum-stances.

I have had my share of difficult situations since I moved to the united - Kingdom from Nigeria and the main difficulty was and still is child care is-sues and coping with a different society moral code. I have since learnt to balance my life, organise my time wisely, save money, study at home and yet remain an active Christian.

What Is God's view on resourcefulness?

In the beginning, God said "let us make man in our own image and likeness"- (Genesis 1:26) He also made the world and everything in it and gave the control over to man because He expected us to have the same attributes in us as He does.

God made us creative beings to dominate everywhere we are

or go. Our limitations only linger as much as we allow them.

Areas of resourcefulness for leaders

Spiritual resourcefulness in prayer: Turn-ing every opportunity, meeting, conversation and visit to prayer. Praying instead of worrying. Read-ing the bible at every chance we get and taking fellowship and communion seriously. Every thoughts and words of prayer counts before God. Nobody can resist the power of prayer. "And he told them a parable to the effect that they ought always to pray and not lose heart" -(**Luke 18:1**).

Time resourcefulness: Good planning, time keeping, time management, organisational skills, avoiding procrastination are all useful resources to a follower and leader. "Making the best use of time because the days are evil" – (*Ephesians 5:16*).

Friendship resourcefulness: choosing our friends wisely and being loyal to them is a noble thing Having the ability to network successfully and maintain good relationships as far as possible over a long period of time or identifying the wrong ones and letting them go for the sake of our life goal. We must learn the art of saying goodbye to some relationships that have become weight to us.

Some people are a blessing when they come into our lives, others are a blessing when they leave us. Resourcefulness helps to establish our presence everywhere in the market place, business groups and communities. It brings out our resilience, courage and the ability to endure. The Israelites were advised by God to go and borrow from their neighbours when they were leaving Egypt, this were the items used in build-ing a temple. I have observed that certain nationalities or a group of people tend to occupy quickly when they migrate to a new country due to this attribute of resourcefulness coupled with hard work. It could also be a matter wisdom and the source of the holy Spirit. person of all times who fed thousands the wisdom for us is The most resourceful is our lord Jesus Christ with a few bits of food.

Gratitude and Loyalty

Gratitude is the backbone of resourcefulness because it brings a good feeling to us and towards others thereby creating a warm atmosphere for ideas to flow. Nobody likes an ingrate who goes around complaining all the time, we are advised by Paul in *1 Thessalonians 5:16* "rejoice always". Life will al-ways throw different things at us but our response will determine how far we go or succeed in life.\

Ruth was a grateful woman in the bible, despite her husband, brother in law and father in law dying she maintained the heart of servant and followed Naomi back to Bethlehem. Ruth was grateful as well as loyal, in her declaration she said "Do not urge me to go leave you or to return from following you, for where you go I will go and where you lodge I will lodge. Your people shall be my people and your God my God".

Through loyalty, Ruth ended up in the lineage of Jesus Christ because she stood by her mother in-law who she saw as her leader. Her loyalty paid off in the end. We live in a world where loyalty is like a bad word and it is a becoming a lonely word.

5

Leading by Faith and Prayer

"Without faith, it is impossi-ble to please God"-
(*Hebrews 11:6*)

Many people accept or conclude that they have faith, but the direction of their faith may begin to change especially when storms of life hits. Faith is not an abstract term but a deep conviction that rests on an agreement between two entities It is an expectation that something or someone will do or be to your advantage. For a follower lead-er, there is an assumption that they have faith in their leader and ultimately in God.

Leadership is a leap of faith into the unknown,

unseen, sometimes unstable and uncontrolled human minefield. Faith must become a leader's life-style; every successful vision is achieved by a level of faith in the leader. Without faith, you can't follow to the end because the road can become long and hard. For a Christian, faith in God is the starting and endpoint of leadership because God holds all the cards and keys. Faith must be coupled with prayer because both are inseparable. If you don't have faith, you won't pray and if you don't pray you may never contact faith.

"Behold, his soul which is lifted up is not upright in him: but the just shall live by his faith" – (*Habakkuk 2:4*)

Leaders and followers need a vibrant faith to conquer the enemy because he will set up obstacles to progress. This will occur at every stage in life and leadership, most of them are usually erected or created by human traditions, wrong motives or pure hatred for change which can potentially put an end to a man's vision. According to Zig Ziglar "When obstacles arise, change your direction to reach your goal not the decision." Having a strong faith in God, knowing our purpose and believing in our vision is the anchor for our ability to trust and not give up when hard times hit. Heroes of faith who passed away could not attribute any of their successes to personal strength but all of them claimed to have faith in a higher and supreme being to keep their vision alive.

The Follower Leader and Obedience

E.M Bounds stated that "I have observed that many followers of Christ struggle with obedience because it is confused with subservience which is the willingness to obey others without questioning. It is not an attitude that the modern day encourages in most of us, we are told to ask questions, give feed-backs, complain, stand for our rights"

There is nothing wrong with speaking up especially as we strive to maintain a just society, however, when it comes to leadership, the best form of learning is through obedience and following instructions that may appear very silly at most times but we are aware that even God uses simple things to teach us and show us that He can do anything with a willing heart. The instructions we refer to are presumed to be based on the scriptures and align with christian values derived from them. God prescribes obedience to follower – leaders among His children. The steps to destiny are carved in the footsteps of leaders, find it and follow it.

The bible describes Elisha in a unique way, "but Jehoshaphat asked Is there no prophet of the LORD here, through whom we may inquire of the LORD? An officer of the king of Israel answered, "Elisha son of Shaphat is here. He used to pour water on the hands of Elijah." - *2 Kings 3:11*.

The bible describes Elisha by the standard of his service not his title, serving others is the gateway to a successful leadership career even when the leader's life profile doesn't fit your personal preference.

Sons of Consolation

Caleb calmed the people before Moses and said, "We must go up and take possession of it, be-cause we are more than able to do it."- But the men who went up with him said, "We can't go up against the people because they are stronger than we." They started a rumour about the land that they had explored, telling the Israelites, "The land that we crossed over to explore is a land that devours its residents. All the people we saw in it are huge men. We saw there the Nephilim the descendants of Anak come from the Nephilim, we saw ourselves as grasshoppers, and that's how we appeared to them. – (*Numbers 13:30-33*).

The entire community raised their voice and the people wept that night. All the Israelites criticized Moses and Aaron. The entire community said to them, "If only we had died in the land of Egypt or if only we had died in this desert! Why is the Lord bringing us to this land to fall by the sword? Our wives and our children will be taken by force.

Wouldn't it be better for us to return to Egypt?" So, they said to each other, "Let's pick a leader and let's go back to Egypt. (**Numbers 14:1-4**). The people were disheartened because of the words of a follower leader who lacked faith and managed to escalate a not so good situation into a full-blown bad news. Many churches and groups have been scattered because of this singular act of little faith. When people are lacking in their person-al faith, leadership positions suffer in their hands because they have not conquered their personal giant – doubt. After seeing the parting of the red sea, how God moved the natural elements on their behalf, the arrangement of the waters to de-part while they walked on dry land, eating manna from heaven, yet, the Israelites developed temporary amnesia and forgot the benefits of God be-cause of the report of mere men. A good Christian leader reminds people of the power that God has. Leaders are to encourage people to have faith in God. If a leader is remotely interested in keeping the faith at all, they must watch who they listen to, because not all men have faith. Counsel and advice must be measured by the standard of God's word, if it falls short of the scriptures and the promises of God for your life, it must be discarded quickly. Faith moves us towards an active engage-ment with destiny.

Faith That Takes Risks

Imagine four lepers helping a kingdom to recover lost goods and grounds. They should normally be hidden, because they are out-casts, but they transformed a whole kingdom by their faith. A leader's faith put into the right action can activate a whole generation of people to follow God and right-eousness.

"and there were four leprous men at the entering in of the gate: and they said one to another, why sit we here until we die? If we say, we will enter the city, then the famine is in the city, and we shall die there: and if we sit still here, we die also. Now therefore come, and let us fall unto the host of the Syrians: if they save us alive, we shall live; and if they kill us, we shall but die…" - (*2 Kings 7:3-20*)

In every country of the world, many leaders have emerged over the centuries yet none of them could have achieved their great feats action can activate a whole generation of people to follow God and right-eousness.

if not faith for can the we power lead of and faith. Only follow by well.

Faith Killers

Bad habits can destroy faith. Bad habits come from deep within our soul, that part of us that is unregenerate, the fleshly emotions, feelings, opin-ions, judgements, prejudices and unchallenged biases. If left unattended or unrenewed, the soul of a man can leads him to hell. Church Leaders may need to con-sider the following statements and reflect on them:

Not everyone in church is holy.
Not everybody in church is there to serve God.
Not everyone in church fears God.

Not everyone in church wants to be changed.
Not everyone wants to give money or time to the church.
Most people prefer to eat from what other people provide.
Not everyone in church likes the pastor.
Not everyone in church came to be a helper.
Not everyone came to pray.
Not everyone in church will receive answers to their prayers.

The only common factor is that God has given to every one a level of faith, how they use it is entirely up to them.

6

Leadership and Vision

"the eye is the light of the body, if your eye is single your body shall be full of light - (*Matthew 6: 22*).

You will never have all the answers but don't live like a question mark. Not everyone is a dreamer, not everybody has a vision. If you want to lead, ask God for a vision then He will make you a follower of the vision of a leader because people follow vision longer than a human being.When you begin to add value to somebody's life,

You will never have all the answers but don't live like a question mark.

your leadership skills begin to emerge. You will

be misunderstood especially when you are gift-ed, and the majority of counsel will prompt you to go and start your own "thing". Make people understand your need to follow. You may slow down for people to understand your vision but don't let them slow your vision down. Trust God entirely with your plans and watch them unfold in their time. Vision is the ability to think about or plan the future with imagination or wisdom. - Dictionary.com

Having or developing vision is paramount to leadership and other areas of our lives, any fol-lower leader without a vision plan may be head-ing for serious trouble because their lives may slip by without them realising it and thus be-come uncontrollable. Having a vision doesn't mean you will carry it out alone or immediately. People usually ask me how they can confirm if the vision they have is from God or flesh? My answer to them is get a vision first, pursue it and along the way, the game might change, and you will end up on God's platform. The bottom line is "what-ever your hand finds to do, do it with all your might" – (*Ecclesiastes 9:10*).

Let us consider the para-graph below "Has God been telling you things He wants to do through you, but you are looking at yourself and thinking, how can this happen? You are saying, 'I don't have the training, the resources, the skill, or the connection and I certainly don't have the strength to accomplish it alone.' If you are wondering how God will bring it all to pass, remember that He will accomplish it! No one else will get the credit. How will it happen? "The holy Spirit will come upon you, and the power of the Most High will overshadow you" – (*Luke 1:35a*).

The Holy Spirit can impregnate you with a vision, inspire you with creative ideas, introduce you to the right people, and empower you to do the job. God had a unique plan for Mary, and He has one for you too. You aren't privileged to see the future and you don't know all that God has in store for you. But He has a plan. After the angel spoke to Mary, notice what she said, "Be it unto me according to thy word"' (*Luke 1:38*). Not ac-cording to your social status, or your job description, or your finances, or what you deserve. No, 'Be it unto me according to thy word!'. Was that easy to say or believe? No, she was taking an extreme risk. To be pregnant and unmarried brought dire consequences in those days. Yet she gave herself willingly to God – and the results were miraculous. And God can do the same for you"- UCB, December 25,2018.

Leadership and Resilience

According to dictionary.com "Resilience is the capacity to recover quickly from difficulty and tough situations Is resilience the same as stubbornness? a bit of both really because a leader needs to have a thick skin. It is also the ability to bear hard times. The main difference between the two is that while resilience is a function of adaptability, stubbornness is a blind, inflexible approach to life and situations.

For you to maintain vision and be a successful leader, you need resilience.

What do you need resilience for? It is needed for a follower leader to be able to withstand negative/criticism. It is much need-ed in the periods of discouragement, survive hard times and resist temptation. A resilient personality in the bible is Joseph, the son of Jacob. He survived, slavery, servitude, lustful attack, in-justice, imprisonment, abandonment but he was brought out to rule with Pharaoh in the end. Resilience is a vital leadership attribute that we must all seek to possess because life will never give us what we expect or demand.

How to build and maintain resilience

a. Cherish social support and interaction

b. Treat problems as a learning process

c. Avoid making a drama out of a crisis

d. Celebrate your successes

e. Develop realistic life goals for guidance and a

f. sense of purpose

g. *Take positive action*

h. *Nurture a positive view of yourself*

i. *Practice self - care*

j. *Avoid burn out, manage your stress*

k. *Recognise and accept you don't have all
the answers*

l. *You can't solve everybody's problem*

m. *Accept that some people's problems will never
go away*

n. *Make kingdom connections and keep them,
don't make God your only friend*

The Leader and the Soul

*The main seat of human issues is in the soul – out of
it proceeds emotional problems that deflates the passion
that we have for everything in life. We are what our soul
is before we become a new creature saved by Christ. Then
our spirit be-comes alive and takes over, however, our soul
is still in us but it is sensual still and controlled* by our

choices and desires coupled with out-side influences, associations and friends. The more we move closer to God by His word, He influences our soul to righteousness.

W. Clement Stone wrote, and I quote "Be careful the environment you choose, for it will shape you, be careful the friends you choose for you will become like them". David's story was a good example, having fought Goliath as a youth and won battles against kingdoms as an adult , he sat at home one evening and let his guard down, his soul longed for another man's wife - Bathsheba, whom he saw when she was taking her evening bath and he coveted her using the power of a king to commit the sin of adultery. The soul of a leader must be monitored closely, and the fruits of the spirit must be developed to overcome the temptation of soulish desires. Gehazi was a soulish follower leader who desired material things more than grace. He was only concerned with the commercial part of the anointing and he got leprosy for his trouble. He completely went against the moral code of his leader, Elisha.

He was never going to get the pow-er that Elisha got by following Elijah because he chose the wrong path to follow.

Gehazi, the servant of Elisha the man of God, said to himself, "My master was too easy on Naaman, this Aramean, by not accepting from him what he brought. As surely as the LORD lives, I will run after him and get something from him." So Gehazi hurried after Naaman. When Naaman saw him running to-ward him, he got down from the chariot to meet him.

"Is every thing all right?"he asked.

"Every thing is allright,"Gehazi answered.

"My master sent me to say, 'Two young men from the company of the prophets have just come to me from the hill country of Ephraim...*2 Kings 5:20-30.*

The Integrity of the Follower Leader

Integrity is the distance between your lips and your life. Any follower leader must work towards this quality always. integrity will lead a man to a full and rich life because there will be no need to cover anything or "get the story right". Learning to live by the truth always creates a habit of personal integrity. David lost his integrity when he had an affair with Uriah's wife and killed him to cover his tracks. He was hoping that the secret will be covered when the husband returned from war be-cause David assumed everybody was as complacent as he was, but Uriah was a man of integrity and he watched the king's gate till morning.

"then David sent to Joab, saying, "Send me Uriah the Hittite." And Joab sent Uriah to David. When

Uriah had come to him, David asked how Joab was doing, and how the people were doing, and how the war prospered. And David said to Uriah, "Go down to your house and wash your feet." So Uriah departed from the king's house, and a gift of food from the king followed him. But Uriah slept at the door of the king's house with all the servants of his lord, and did not go down to his house. So when they told David, saying, "Uriah did not go down to his house," David said to Uriah, "Did you not come from a journey? Why did you not go down to your house..." - (*2 Samuel 11:6-13*)

Integrity goes beyond what we do while other people can see us, it is what we do when people are not watching us for instance, as Christians when we make a vow to the lord in secret, integrity will make us pay it but that is not the case for many followers. Integrity must be actively taught to followers and leaders. It must be encouraged and practised because it is not a spiritual gift.

Integrity goes beyond what we do while other people can see us

NOTES

_____
_____
_____
_____
_____
_____
_____
_____
_____
_____
_____
_____
_____
_____
_____
_____
_____
_____
_____
_____
_____
_____

7

The Challenges of the Follower Leader

"Today a reader, tomorrow a leader" - Margaret Fuller, (1810-1850).

Read! Read!! Read!!!

Reading is one of the greatest experiences a human-beings can go through because when we read, we are transformed gradually in our mind and the way we conceptualise. We stop be-ing alone in our pain and groanings. We experience a mirror effect, when we read because what is inside us is reflected by somebody some-where and somehow, we connect with them,

Reading a good book is like visiting another city without the need for a ticket or a visa. It enriches our thoughts, challenges perception and reflects our inner most prejudice even when they are well hidden. A good book transforms the way we view the world and our life issues. From the pages of a book, we can learn about the battles others fight and how they overcame or lost their fights.

There are tremendous treasures hidden in the pages of a book when we decide to read. In my opinion, the best book anybody is privileged to read is the Bible, because in it we discover answers to life 's questions.

Our mind opens when we read books constantly. To ignore reading books is to al-low self - inflicted ignorance and darkness.

In the first year of his reign I, Daniel under-stood by books the number of the years, where-of the word of the LORD came to Jeremiah the prophet, that he would accomplish seventy years in the desolations of Jerusalem (**Daniel 9:2**).

Good books train our minds. The ability to focus is the main benefit in book reading because the mind stays on one subject at a time and you there is nobody else to interrupt the connection.

Even Jesus Christ had to read and study to understand the reason why He came to the world.

"So He came to Nazareth, where He had been brought up. And as His custom was, He went into the synagogue on the Sabbath day, and stood up to read. And He was handed the book of the prophet Isaiah. And when He had opened the book, He found the place where it was written...- (*Luke 6:16-20*).

FEAR OF REJECTION AND CRITICISM

Criticism is like a torch, always pointing in the opposite direction. It is the window to the minds of others for you to see what they think about you. Use their comments as a spring board and soar higher. Criticism only at-tacks your emotions, it can't stop your dream. The only person who can stop it is YOU. Fight rejection with encouragement in the word of God. Encouragers are few, but they still exist. Make friends with them and hold on to them when you find them. They are usually quieter than others and won't speak in the crowd. They don't take on big assignments but will respond to acts of kindness when you suggest it to them. Don't over-look them.

Offence

Annoyance or resentment brought about by a perceived insult to or disregard for oneself. Any follower leader who has a clear vision must learn to recognise offence, refuse to be offended and keep their dreams in view.' Offence is a huge distraction and results only in bitterness. I have had hundreds of instances in my life that could have offended me but I know enough through the study of the bible that my inner man must be subjected to God totally because man may make mistakes about me, but God doesn't make mistakes whatever He says I will become will come to pass if I open my heart to Him alone. Any follower leader that allows offence into their hearts may be playing with a deadly poison that eradicates vison because offence will poison your spirit and will not allow you to see the good in any situation.

My final charge: Then he said to the crowd, "If any of you wants to be my follower, you must turn from your selfish ways, take up your cross daily, and follow me.

ABOUT THE AUTHOR

Kemi Adesola is an active member of the body of Christ in the UK. She lives in Edinburgh Scotland with her husband and children.

She is into mentoring, counselling and coaching people on how to develop their talents, potentials and visions as they grow in a constantly changing and challenging world.

She is passionate about teaching self confidence and a positive self image that is derived from the true and consistent knowledge of the Bible.

She likes to travel and also support charitable events and causes.

NOTES

NOTES

_____
_____
_____
_____
_____
_____
_____
_____
_____
_____
_____
_____
_____
_____
_____
_____
_____
_____
_____
_____
_____
_____

Printed in Great Britain
by Amazon